C000134650

DERBY
THEN & NOW
IN COLOUR

MAXWELL CRAVEN

The
History
Press

Dedicated to Robert Innes-Smith

First published 2011

The History Press
The Mill, Brimscombe Port
Stroud, Gloucestershire, GL5 2QG
www.thehistorypress.co.uk

© Maxwell Craven, 2011

The right of Maxwell Craven to be identified as the Author
of this work has been asserted in accordance with the
Copyrights, Designs and Patents Act 1988.

All rights reserved. No part of this book may be reprinted
or reproduced or utilised in any form or by any electronic,
mechanical or other means, now known or hereafter invented,
including photocopying and recording, or in any information
storage or retrieval system, without the permission in writing
from the Publishers.

British Library Cataloguing in Publication Data.
A catalogue record for this book is available from the British Library.

ISBN 978 0 7524 6348 3

Typesetting and origination by The History Press
Production managed by Jellyfish Print Solutions and manufactured in India

CONTENTS

ACKNOWLEDGEMENTS

Much of the research that has gone into the captions that follow was accumulated over thirty years, and I thus owe a debt of gratitude to all my former colleagues at Derby Museum, many of whom have told me things I didn't know, and especially to the staff, past and present, of the Derby Local Studies Library, who have always been so tolerant and helpful.

My heartfelt thanks for the loan of pictures and for information are due to many friends and acquaintances as well as those kind people who read my twice-weekly historical column in the *Derby Evening Telegraph* and have volunteered pictures and information in prodigious quantities.

If the following list is not complete, then to anyone omitted I submit my most abject apologies: Michael Allseybrook of Ashton Antiques, Peter Billson, Alan and Clive Champion, James Darwin, Don Farnsworth, Stuart Gillis and his colleagues at the Derby Museum, Olga Fraser, Frank Gilbert, Don Gwinnett, the late Roy Hughes, Robert Innes-Smith, Derek Jewell, Nigel Kirk, James Lewis, Roger Pegg, Gerald Redfern, Rose Robinson, the late Sir Reresby Sitwell Bt, Sheila Tarling, Michael Willis and Peggy Withington.

I am also most grateful to my former colleagues at the *Derby Evening Telegraph* for always being so helpful, even though I hardly ever used to see them! Finally, to my wife Carole, for forbearance, tolerance, the application to my needs of her superb driving skills and her critical eye, for all of which I am in her debt and to whom I offer my thanks and appreciation.

ABOUT THE AUTHOR

Maxwell Craven is an author, historian, conservation lobbyist and graduate of the University of Nottingham. He is the author of numerous books mainly on architecture, biography and local history, including a monograph on John Whitehurst FRS. He was awarded an honorary degree by the University of Derby (1996) and was elected FSA and appointed MBE in 1999.

INTRODUCTION

The title *Derby Then & Now* implies change and the contents show it, for Derby has had more than its share. It changed radically between the end of the Second World War and the early 1970s, yet the boom years from the mid 1990s until 2008 led to further changes on an even more far-reaching scale. The main culprit in both periods was the building of the Inner Ring Road (1966–71) from the north-west to the east of the city and 2007–11, when the remainder was completed. Radical transformations wrought on some historic townscapes by this road – by no means universally welcomed nor particularly effective in completion – have been highly deleterious and have opened the way to further intrusive new developments, of which the Riverlights and Jury's Inn along with two others have been approved (but not yet built) for Full Street and off Friar Gate.

Derby began as a small Roman walled town – Derventio (modern Little Chester) – which was re-occupied by the Vikings in 874, and a separate Saxon minster church, built nearby probably in the eighth century, which were both absorbed into a Saxon fortified town established in 921 and which by 1066 boasted 200 or so burgesses, eight or nine churches (two of which were minsters), several mills and a mint. Derby was long acknowledged as a fine, well-built county town, and by the eighteenth century had attracted a large number of fine houses, built by the lead- and coal-rich gentry for their town residences. These men sponsored the Derby Assembly Rooms (the interior decorated by Robert Adam, now demolished) and their wealth enabled new, luxury industries to flourish: the Silk Mill (England's first factory, 1718), the china factory, the spar manufactory, John Whitehurst's clockworks, Jedediah Strutt's calico mills and a foundry specialising in ornamental ironwork.

Derby was home to two of the founders of the celebrated Lunar Society, John Whitehurst and Dr Erasmus Darwin; their influence on the industrial revolution both locally and nationally was incalculable, quite apart from the artists and craftsmen they and the other gentry sponsored: the painter Joseph Wright, ARA, the architect Joseph Pickford, the landscaper William Emes and others.

The patronage of many facets of Derby's life thereafter by William Strutt, the son of cotton pioneer Jedediah, swept the borough into the industrial age. A great rebuilding and an expansion with (generally) good quality artisans' housing, was supported by a succession of Improvement Commissions, all but one chaired by Strutt, set up by statute between 1768 and 1829.

The coming of the railway to Derby in 1839 provided further stimulus, including the diversification of the foundries into heavy engineering, the widening of the main streets (recorded from 1854 by pioneer photographer Richard Keene (1825–94), some of whose photographs are included in this book), and the rapid improvement in the provision of education and other facilities for Derby's population, which rose from 8,000 in the later eighteenth century to 240,000 today.

The twentieth century saw the establishment of Rolls-Royce in 1907 – the last of the great foundries and, as a car-maker, the last of Derby's luxury industries – the elevation of the town into a city (1977), the coming of a university (1992) and the broadening of the industrial base from railway engineering and aero-engines, into a thriving, diverse and prosperous settlement. The cost to the built environment could have been worse, but a real understanding and regard for the city's heritage has not been a strong point among its elected representatives.

THE MARKET PLACE

Nos 2 AND 3 Market Place, looking north-east, photographed by Richard Keene, *c*.1865. The former was rebuilt after a fire in March 1741 and was converted into a town house in 1763 by lead merchant William Cox of Brailsford Hall. A branch of his family later used it as a wine merchant's, taken over by Messrs Pountain, and it was replaced in 1889 by a building

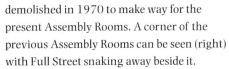

demolished in 1970 to make way for the present Assembly Rooms. A corner of the previous Assembly Rooms can be seen (right) with Full Street snaking away beside it.

APPROXIMATELY THE SAME scene today. To the left stands the 1923 War Memorial, designed by Charles Clayton Thompson (1873–1932) and carved by A.G. Walker, ARA. The entire scene, once intimate and Georgian, is now dominated by Sir Hugh Casson's vast Assembly Rooms (opened 1977). The Palladian stone façade of the former Assembly Rooms survived to be taken to Crich Tramway Museum for re-erection. The huge television screen was inaugurated in 2008, underwritten by Derby University. No one seems to watch it.

DERBY'S GUILDHALL

A DETAIL FROM a view of the south side of the Market Place in 1828 by George Pickering. The sumptuous baroque Guildhall of 1731 is featured, with a view of Corn Market between it and the south-east angle of the Piazzas of 1708. The architect of the Guildhall was Richard Jackson of Armitage (1703–51), and it was demolished in the same year as this view was drawn when a plot on the south side became available on which to build afresh. John Whitehurst supplied the clock, earning himself the freedom to trade.
(*Reproduced courtesy of Derby Museum*)

THE PRESENT GUILDHALL replaced a short-lived Neo-Greek one designed by Matthew Habershon, built in 1828 and which burnt down on Trafalgar Day 1841. What one sees today is a drastic 1842 rebuilding by Henry Duesbury, grandson of the founder of the Derby China Factory, with a tower and a pair of bas-relief panels by John Bell (1812–96). It is shown in the modern photograph on the right from the east to demonstrate a startling contrast with the newly completed Quad Arts building, opened in 2008.

IRON GATE AND
MARKET HEAD

THE VIEW DOWN Iron Gate to Sadler Gate and Rotten Row, as recorded by Richard Keene in May 1855 (left). Until 1784 a wooden beam crossed the street from the light stuccoed building next to the horse. In that year the beam collapsed, killing a horse; it once bore the ornate sign of the George Inn, which became defunct in 1814. The building to the right, nearest the camera, is the Talbot Inn (closed and demolished 1877); three bays of the next building were replaced in the 1950s. Everything on the left went in 1866.
(*Reproduced courtesy of Derby Museum*)

IN 1992 THE street was pedestrianised and given ersatz 'heritage' lighting standards and bollards. The pillar, with its metal astrolabe-like finial, was erected the same year in honour of the painter Joseph Wright, ARA (1734–97), and was situated outside the building that replaced his parental home.

IRON GATE AND THE
CATHEDRAL TOWER

A RECENTLY DISCOVERED Richard Keene photograph of Iron Gate (left), taken from outside the Talbot Inn with Keene's own shop next door. This was at the time when he had also taken No. 24, a little further up (out of shot), adding a gallery on the roof to display his photographs. The end shop on the right was designed by George Henry Sheffield. The street in front of the cathedral had been widened, dating the view to between 1873 and 1880. Note the spire of St Alkmund's in the distance, behind the cathedral tower.

BY APRIL 2011, 126 years later, Keene's printing shop and the Talbot Inn have long since vanished, to be replaced by the former Crompton & Evans Union Bank (later NatWest), itself converted into a pub called the Standing Order. The adjacent early eighteenth-century building, which was once Brigden's gents' outfitters, was severely butchered when it was converted into a Yates's Wine Lodge in 1997; the garden front was virtually obliterated.

THE CATHEDRAL CENTRE

NOS 18–19 IRON GATE, 1872 (right).
J. Hives, grocer, and Edwin Cooling,
seedsman and florist, occupy a building
put up as part of a development that
extended some way down St Mary's Gate
(to the right of the photograph). This was
constructed in 1800–2 and financed by
Mrs Richardson, the widow of a banker,
almost as a modern 'property development',
although the grandest house in the St
Mary's Gate part was her own residence. The
architect was probably John Welch of Derby
(1759–1823). Richard Keene (whose gallery
can be seen on the building on the far left)
took the picture on 17 December 1872, with
the street bedecked for the visit of HRH the
Prince of Wales.
(*Reproduced courtesy of Derby Museum*)

THE SAME SCENE in April 2011(left), and remarkably little has changed. Messrs Clulow, a much-esteemed bookshop that occupied the site for four generations, closed in 1998, its demise hastened by the coming of Waterstone's. The building was then acquired by the cathedral chapter and converted into Derby Cathedral Centre thanks to the inspiration of the dean, Michael Perham, now bishop of Gloucester. It was opened by HM the Queen on 14 November 2003.

ST MARY'S GATE: A CLASSIC VIEW

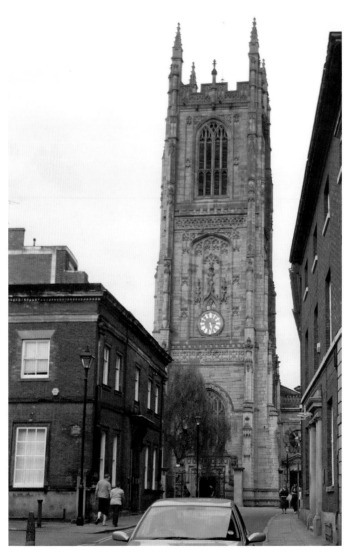

UPPER ST MARY'S GATE, *c.*1895 (right). Whichever way you view the cathedral and its tower, it never fails to impress. St Mary's Gate, named after a long-vanished medieval church, was once packed with elegant town houses, the grandest of which, St Mary's Gate House of about 1732, hides behind its Palladian screen and Bakewell gates. Mrs Richardson's house of 1802 is on the right in both views.

THE LOSS OF St Mary's Gate House to make more room for Kenning's in 1938 caused an ugly gap (on the left edge). The house beyond, Robotham's solicitors, is all that remains following the widening of Queen Street, which led to the demolition of the buildings beyond and their replacement by a new office block, set well back. It was during its construction that vestiges of the lost St Mary's church were found. The only modern change will be the planned building of an office block, part of which will obtrude into the gap where St Mary's Gate House once stood. One can only hope it will do justice to an elegant street. The wrought-iron gates in front of the cathedral (by Robert Bakewell) were moved from St Mary's Gate House.

DARLEY ABBEY

DARLEY ABBEY, 1971. From the top of Duffield Road one descends into Darley Abbey, an almost perfectly preserved, largely Regency mill village. Until 1538 it was the county's largest

monastery, but on the Dissolution it was converted into a country house. This building, seen here in a state of collapse after over a century divided as artisans' cottages, is thought to be the only substantial surviving abbey building, albeit of unknown purpose. (*Reproduced courtesy of Don Farnsworth*)

DARLEY ABBEY, APRIL 2011 (above). Derby architect Richard Wood finally succeeded in acquiring the building, convincing the locals that they wanted a pub after 150 years without one (the natives wanted one, the incomers didn't!) and getting the necessary permissions sorted out. In the end he managed to convert the building with some panache into the Abbey Inn. It opened on 5 October 1979 and has proved a great success.

THE DERBY SILK MILL

DERBY SILK MILL, photographed by Richard Keene, *c*.1865 (right). This atmospheric image of a glassy calm Derwent was taken from the point where the Darley extension of the Derby Canal once debouched into the river by J. & G. Haywood's Phoenix Foundry. The mill was gutted by fire in 1821, and in rebuilding acquired its distinctive arcaded tower (the twin of one provided by William Strutt's friend Kirk Boott on one of his mills at Lowell, Massachusetts, USA) and hipped roof. The chimney marks the impending replacement of waterpower by steam.

THE PHOTOGRAPHER'S POSITION in the old photograph is now occupied by the Causey Bridge, which carries the 1968 inner ring road over the Derwent. The mill itself is now lower, having again been gutted by fire in 1910 and rebuilt with only three storeys. At that time Alderman Unwin Sowter's bakery, corn and maltings firm (successors of William Brown's) was also burnt out. After the fire they added a large mill to the northern end. The weir has long gone and a distinct greening of the riverbank has taken place. Derby City Council bought the freehold of the Silk Mill from the nationalised electricity undertaking when the lease ran out, ensuring the future of the building. The mill is now the southernmost point in the Derwent Valley Mills World Heritage Site.

THE RIVER DERWENT

THE DERWENT'S WEST bank looking north from Exeter Bridge, from an anonymous Calotype photograph dated 1855. Left of centre is the spire of St Alkmund's church, founded in the seventh century and demolished in 1967, and the tower of Pugin's Church of St Mary (1838–44). To the right is the Derby Silk Mill (1718), five storeys high, with its Regency arcaded tower. Towards the centre of the view is the three-storey doubling shop, which collapsed in September 1890. The gardens of the once elegant town houses (left) have been covered by industrial buildings. (*Reproduced courtesy of Derby Museum*)

THE SAME VIEW today (above). Following a fire in 1910, the Silk Mill was rebuilt, but only three storeys high. The building has been the Derby Industrial Museum since 1974. The late lamented Derby Urban Regeneration Company initiated the landscaping inbetween, including the intrusive (and little used) new footbridge. The footbridge serves two half-empty blocks of flats built on the east bank in 2007, which were permitted to rise to the same height as Derby Silk Mill tower. Dominating the scene, and hiding Pugin's Church of St Mary, is the twelve-storey Jury's Inn, allowed by the council in 2006 against the advice of English Heritage and all the amenity societies.

DERBY COUNCIL HOUSE

THE CENTREPIECE OF the 1931 Central Improvement Plan was the Derby Council House, which was only a shell when the Second World War broke out, and was immediately requisitioned. It was later completed without much of the intended detail (which included a

stone pylon above its grand pedimented entrance) and with only utility furniture within, giving the mayor's reception suite a spartan air. For all that it is still a tour de force of a building. The river arch marks the outfall of the culverted Markeaton Brook, the higher one (left) a link to a separate intended council chamber. This is one of architect C.H. Alsin's perspectives. *(Reproduced with permission of His Worship the Mayor of Derby)*

THE SAME SCENE in April 2011 (above) has barely changed – for now. Aslin designed the serpentine stepped riverbank to set the building off and to embellish the Riverside Gardens, laid out as a memorial to the fallen of the Great War. They have now been partially sacrificed to build Riverlights. The Council House itself is about to be rebuilt to increase its accommodation without seriously affecting its mass, hence the boarded-up windows. Unfortunately, the architect was allowed to take a full-height chunk out of the south wall, seemingly more for effect than efficacy.

MORLEDGE FAIR

THE PAINTING BELOW is called 'The Morledge, Derby, in Fair Time, 1882' and is by gentleman amateur Revd Charles Thomas Moore of Appleby Parva (d. 1922). Although not technically of

the first rank, it is a very jolly and largely accurate account of the Morledge from Cockpit Hill. In the left distance, below the cupola of the Guildhall, are Tower Buildings, which are still standing; the centre is dominated by the shot tower, built in 1809 by Cox Bros, lead merchants, with All Saints' tower behind St Alkmund's and Alderman Robert Pegg's colour works. (*Derby Museum, Goodey Collection No. 352*)

IN 1972 COCKPIT Hill, the point of view of the painting, was cleared for the erection of the Eagle Centre Market, rebuilt in 1991 and incorporated into Westfield in 2008, part of which is visible (above, extreme left). The shot tower went in 1931 and the paint works a year later, to be replaced in 1933 by the Open Market and bus station, themselves replaced respectively by the Crown Court (1988, just visible, right) and Riverlights (2010). The only surviving points of reference are the tower of the Guildhall (just left of the late nineteenth-century Tower Buildings, left, middle distance) and the cathedral's 172ft tower, rising from the grim bulk of the Quad building.

TWO NEW BUS STATIONS

DERBY BUS STATION, *c.*1935. In place of the colour works of Alderman Pegg, Herbert Aslin built a state-of-the-art bus station, which, because of the constrictions of the site, had to be laid out on a parabolic plan. The internal arrangement was derived from railway practice and was said to have been based on an example in the New World. The style was unashamedly moderne, the terminal building being a drum externally decorated with reliefs, with a marble-sheathed circulating hall, café, enquiry office, etc., between symmetrical wings containing retail units in canted bays. It had a

good capacity and worked well from an operational point of view. Note the vast fleet of idle buses parked behind, right.

DERBY BUS STATION, 2011 (above). A plan was hatched in 1995 to build a vast retail, casino, bus station and prestige housing development on the site of the old bus station, in conjunction with Metro-Holst. A brash, multi-coloured glass design was approved, but little happened, all efforts to save the innovatively planned old bus station failed, and in the end, with the old facility flattened, Metro-Holst went bust, and everything stalled. The scheme was eventually rescued, but finished in a much simplified form, the bulk of the hideously unlovely new development containing two hotels, and finished in battleship grey. The bus station, too, leaves much to be desired, with some operators choosing to ignore it. The protuberance in the road is a piece of 'public art'.

THE OLD DERBY
CHINA FACTORY

A DERBY TEACUP, decorated with a view of the Derby China Factory of about 1800 can be seen in the photograph above. Derby's Nottingham Road has never been a showpiece, but it was the location, for almost a century, of the Derby China Factory, which was founded in about 1750. No other authentic view of the works survives, save a drawing done from memory by Moses Webster almost forty years after its demise, another speculative view and some enigmatic architects' drawings in the local collection, one being of a weighbridge house by

Joseph Pickford. There was intense interest, therefore, when this cup surfaced in a sale in Derby in 1999.
(*Reproduced courtesy of Neales*)

APPROXIMATELY THE SAME scene today can be seen below, dominated by the Derby Inner Ring Road (begun 1965, finished 2011), running on an elevated plinth 10ft in front of the windows of the surviving eighteenth-century cottages which once abutted the china factory. The three-storey building was once the Punch Bowl inn of 1758, which closed in 1908 due to pressure on the bench from the Temperance movement. It once had a sizeable cockpit at the rear with elevated seating to one side, the former now incorporated into a round kitchen and the latter forming a mezzanine to the rear; a rare survival.

LOWER ST PETER'S STREET

LOWER ST PETER'S STREET. This Keene view of the east side of the street north of East Street below shows it virtually unchanged since the eighteenth century. Edward Johnson, a prolific clockmaker,

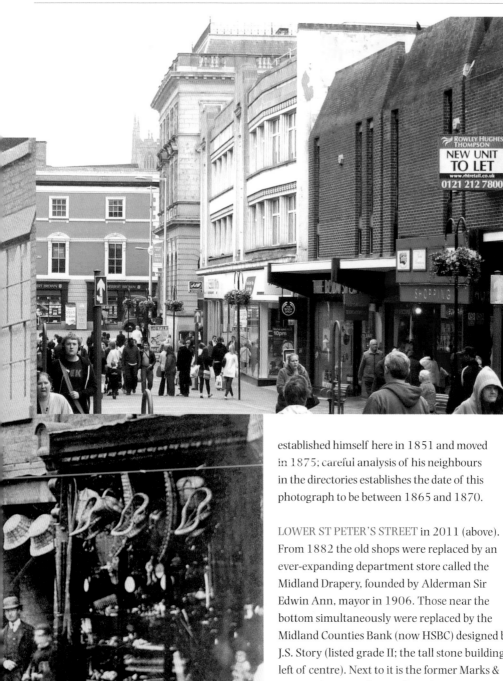

established himself here in 1851 and moved in 1875; careful analysis of his neighbours in the directories establishes the date of this photograph to be between 1865 and 1870.

LOWER ST PETER'S STREET in 2011 (above). From 1882 the old shops were replaced by an ever-expanding department store called the Midland Drapery, founded by Alderman Sir Edwin Ann, mayor in 1906. Those near the bottom simultaneously were replaced by the Midland Counties Bank (now HSBC) designed by J.S. Story (listed grade II; the tall stone building left of centre). Next to it is the former Marks & Spencer (1936 and 1952 by Robert Lutyens) now Tesco Express and, nearest the camera (to the right of the photograph) is part of the dreary 1972 Audley Centre which replaced the Midland Drapery.

ST PETER'S CHURCH

ST PETER'S CHURCH, 1860s. St Peter's Street did not need widening until one reached the church.
G. Gordon Place of Nottingham rebuilt the church in 1851–53 (adding a big new vicarage
further up the Burton Road), but the widening and replacement churchyard wall were done in

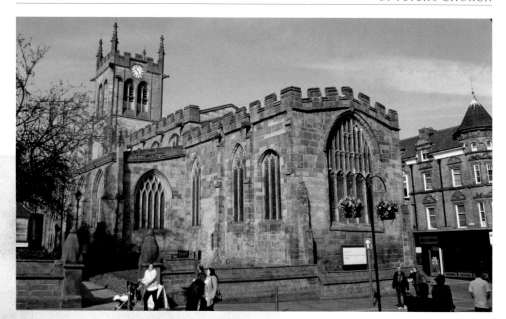

1858–59 along with a restoration of the chancel by Derby architect John Price (1795–1859); as the rotunda building just beyond the church (see above, right) was not erected until 1879, the photograph from which this heliotype was taken must date to between 1859 and 1878, but probably in the 1860s.

ST PETER'S CHURCH, 2011. The church underwent further rebuildings. While Price was reworking the chancel, the remainder was receiving a 'sensitive restoration' by George Edmund Street (which doesn't say much for the durability of Place's work!). Indeed, Price's work is what survives, nearest the camera, for the whole of the rest of the church was taken down and rebuilt by the little-known John Hawley Lloyd of Birmingham in 1897–98 – note how the tower has changed. It was then that the old clock (allegedly by ironsmith Robert Bakewell) was replaced by one made by Smith of Derby, along with a new dial.

THE OLD GRAMMAR
SCHOOL

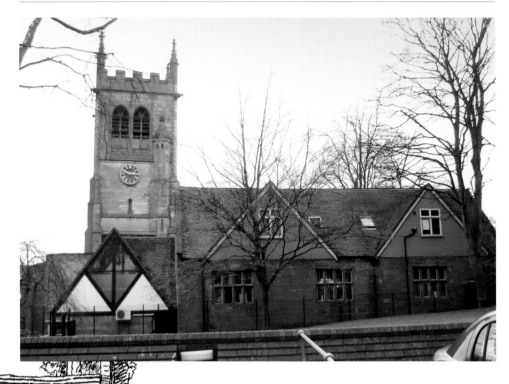

AN INK DRAWING of St Peter's churchyard in the 1840s (left). G. Gordon Place's restoration of St Peter's church took place just a few months before Keene took his first photographs, so this drawing is the only record of the tower as it was previously, with its off-centre louvered lancets with their almost Saxon stone framing. In front is Derby (Grammar) School, still then in use, founded by charter in 1555, although the building would appear to date from some fifty years later. The cottages bounding the north side of the churchyard (then not a thoroughfare) belonged to the Liversage charity.

ST PETER'S CHURCHYARD, April 2011 (above). Today the scene is not radically different. The old grammar school is still there, with the church behind, albeit with Mr Lloyd's tower in succession to Place's effort (see page p. 35). In about 1973 Derek Montague added the modernist portico to the school when it became Raymond's studios. After some years as a commercial heritage centre it is now the hairdressing emporium of the architect's daughter. Yet just off to the right is a huge concrete office block on Gower Street. How long this small sward will remain undeveloped it is impossible to say.

THE BOTTOM OF
BABINGTON LANE

A POSTCARD VIEW of St Peter's Street north from the junction with Babington Lane, 1905.
The building on the corner occupies the site of the early Tudor gatehouse of Babington Hall,

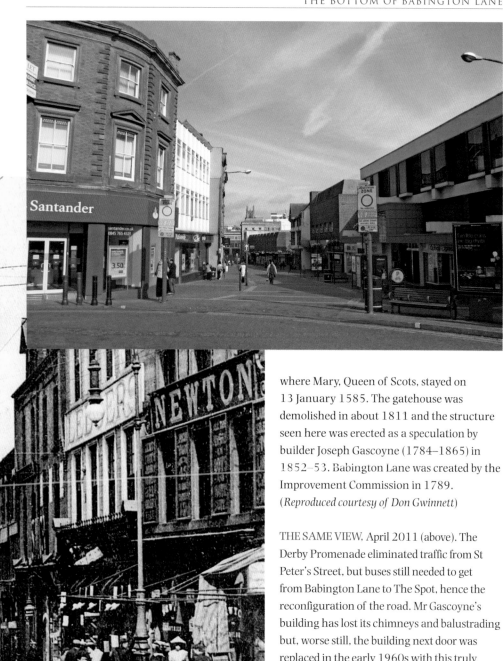

where Mary, Queen of Scots, stayed on 13 January 1585. The gatehouse was demolished in about 1811 and the structure seen here was erected as a speculation by builder Joseph Gascoyne (1784–1865) in 1852–53. Babington Lane was created by the Improvement Commission in 1789. (*Reproduced courtesy of Don Gwinnett*)

THE SAME VIEW, April 2011 (above). The Derby Promenade eliminated traffic from St Peter's Street, but buses still needed to get from Babington Lane to The Spot, hence the reconfiguration of the road. Mr Gascoyne's building has lost its chimneys and balustrading but, worse still, the building next door was replaced in the early 1960s with this truly dire glass and concrete white-painted building constructed for a building society. On the east side nearly everything has been replaced (mainly in the 1970s) and it is notable that the new build is, without exception, low and mean, wrecking the street scene.

THE SPOT

THE SPOT IS a name unknown before 1741 for the junction of London Road (turnpiked in the 1750s) and Osmaston Road; its origin is utterly obscure. Maltster Abraham Ward may have first coined this name for his own premises: was the four-bay three-storey curved building situated on the inside of the junction the original Spot? This pre-1904 lithographic postcard (below) shows the

streetscape barely changed since Ward's day, bar the large shop on the far right, built in 1897–98.

IN 1906 A fine statue of Queen Victoria by Charles Bell Birch was erected in the centre of the view (a gift of Alderman Sir Alfred Haslam) but was moved to the grounds of the Derbyshire Royal Infirmary in 1928 when found to be too heavy for the new public loos installed beneath it! In 1934 the moderne building on the inside of the angle was built to designs by Sir Frederick Bennett and Partners and in 1991 a clock tower (clock by Smith of Derby Ltd) was built on the site of the statue. The high roof behind is that of the former Gaumont Palace cinema, later a night club, currently empty.

THE SPOT CONTINUED

THE SPOT FROM London Road, photographed by Richard Keene on the occasion of a visit from HRH Edward, Prince of Wales, 15 July 1881. The street was decorated with a floral arch paid for out of the deep pockets of Alderman Sir Abraham Woodiwiss (1828–84), then mayor for the second successive time – doubtless re-elected in the knowledge that he would be generous!

Through the right arch is Babington House (formerly Sitwell Hall), built by the borough's first ever mayor, Henry Mellor, in 1626. By this date its forecourt had been infilled with shops.
(*Reproduced courtesy of Derby Museums*)

IT IS A measure of the drastic manner in which the angle on the left was cut back in 1911 that Babington Buildings – erected in 1897–98 to designs of Methodist chapel architect John Wills for Councillor Fletcher of the Public Benefit Boot & Shoe Company and now Waterstone's – stand to the far right of this scene. The 1991 clock tower is invisible behind its two art deco-style outliers – colloquially known as the 'gun emplacements' – and to the right everything has been replaced twice since 1881, and is currently the western extremity of the 2008 Westfield Shopping Centre. The two column-like objects were intended by Westfield to be 'vertical flower beds' but have so far failed to bloom!

LONDON ROAD

LONDON ROAD VIEWED from the corner of
Bradshaw Street (right) after the demolition
of the graceful Swedenborgian chapel of
1819 for the large block of shops (centre
of the photograph) in 1902 and before
electrification of the tramways in July 1904.
The pedimented building is H.I. Stevens's
Congregational chapel of 1846 on the corner
of Traffic Street.
(*Reproduced courtesy of Don Gwinnett*)

NOTHING COULD BE more drastic than the
effects of the Westfield development and the
1938 part of the Ring Road on the 1903 view.
The chapel, after conversion into a cinema in
1934, was demolished in order to widen the

intersection with Traffic Street in 1962; the rest were replaced by a new shopping precinct called Main Centre in the same year and that, in its turn, was demolished to build Westfield's gigantic retail complex in 2004–8. The bridge connects the Westfield Car Park, an extension of which is on the west side of the street.

DERBY TRIJUNCT STATION

AN ENGRAVING OF Derby station, *c.*1843, can be seen below. The station was built in 1839 for the three companies that amalgamated in 1844 to form the Midland Railway, and was designed by the North Midland Railway's architect, Francis Thompson (1808–95). All three shared one enormously long platform. On the right here is Thompson's Midland Hotel, which was built by London contractor Thomas Jackson on his own initiative and opened on 1 June 1841.

THE STATION, DESPITE rebuilding in 1871 (by J.H. Sanders) and 1892–93 (by Charles Trubshaw), was essentially untouched behind its accretions, but in 1984 British Rail decided to replace it, and after English Heritage pusillanimously refused to list it, its fate was sealed. The replacement was described by Gavin Stamp in a SAVE report of the time as a 'meretricious high tech shack'. Fortunately, the Grade II listed Midland Hotel survives (right), albeit unnecessarily renamed the Heritage Hotel. The new station is soon to have a huge glass porte cochère added to it.

ROLLS-ROYCE

ROLLS-ROYCE WORKS, 1913 (right). The company moved to Derby from Manchester in 1907, having acquired a substantial chunk of the former Osmaston Hall estate on the west side of Osmaston Road at a very reasonable price. The works were opened in 1908, and the 380ft long 'commercial block' – designed personally by Sir Henry Royce and built by Andrew Handyside & Co. of Duke Street – was completed in the autumn of 1912. Royce designed the sills of the three- and four-light mullioned windows awkwardly high, so that people working in the offices could not see out from their desks and be distracted from their work! The Mess House in the foreground was built in 1910.

IN 1937–38 THE company, frequently host of parties for high-ranking dignitaries, often from abroad, put in a bravura art deco centrepiece in Portland stone. The interior was lavishly decorated with marble and, thereafter, became universally known as the Marble Hall. The old 'centre' of the building (at bay sixteen out of thirty-six) had been a cramped, double staircase but thereafter the building had much more *gravitas*. At the same time the entire block was widened at the rear. In 2009 Rolls-Royce abandoned the site for redevelopment, but fortunately, the Derbyshire Archaeological Society managed to get the main building Grade II listed. Presently it stands empty, awaiting a new purpose; everything behind it has been cleared.

ENGLAND'S FIRST PUBLIC PARK

THE ARBORETUM, 1907. John Claudius Loudon (1783–1843) laid out this 11-acre public park for the philanthropical cotton manufacturer Joseph Strutt in 1840. Most of the buildings are by Edward Buckton Lamb, but the Orangery (left of centre) with the entrance lodge on its other side, dates from 1853 and is the work of Henry Duesbury (d. 1872). The houses in the square beyond

were by Charles Humphreys. The park itself was scattered with pieces of sculpture from Strutt's own garden, including the terracotta copy of the Florentine Boar by William John Coffee (1773–1846), right.

THE ARBORETUM, APRIL 2011(above). Time, industrial pollution and the Second World War 'dig for victory' campaign did nothing for Loudon's design, and, in addition, many of the sculptures were either stolen or melted down for scrap in the war. The boar itself was smashed by shrapnel from the Victorian bandstand when it received a direct hit from a bomb. The Derbyshire Historic Buildings Trust restored the Orangery as photographers' studios in 1991, and a lottery grant has been obtained to restore the rest. A replacement boar was made in bronze by a local metalworker and reinstated on the original site.

ROYAL CROWN DERBY

ROYAL CROWN DERBY factory, photographed by W. Morrell in 1936 (right). In 1839 a site next to the Arboretum was selected to erect a Union Workhouse for Derby and Litchurch, then two separate local authorities. The architect was John Mason of Derby (1794–1847). In 1877 a larger new workhouse was opened on Uttoxeter Road, and the old one acquired by the newly founded Crown Derby Company ('Royal' only from 1889), keen to make fine china in Derby. In 1878–79 it was adapted by H.I. Stevens's former partner, Frederick Josias Robinson (1834–92), who added the fine portico and tower with a cast-aluminium corona – one of the earliest architectural uses of this metal in the UK.

THE FACTORY IN April 2011 (left). The factory (which ensured the continuity of china-making in Derby by taking over the King Street factory in 1935) was acquired by Royal Doulton in 1969. The company immediately pulled down the centrepiece and replaced it as here, retaining the cupola, which was refurbished in the 1980s. Subsequently, UPVC windows have done Mason's surviving structure no favours aesthetically, but the firm is now independent again under the management of the Hon. Hugh Gibson and the chairmanship of Roger Boissier CBE. (*Reproduced courtesy of Peter Billson*)

OSMASTON ROAD

OSMASTON ROAD, SOUTH, from
outside Wilderslow, photographed
by W.W. Winter of Midland Road in
early afternoon on a hot summer
day in 1911 (right). An open-topped
electric tram heads for the town
centre, with the ornately Gothic
Melbourne House on the right, built
in 1863–64 for Alderman Robert
Pegg, the paint manufacturer; the
architect was Thomas Chambers Hine
of Nottingham (1813–99). The area
was then an extremely fashionable
early Victorian suburb, part of the
autonomous Litchurch until 1879.

THE SCENE HAS changed remarkably
little in a century. It is late morning
on a hot summer day (above) and
the view suffers from being unable to

match the depth of field of that from 1911. Melbourne House has been much mauled internally and neglected externally thanks to having been acquired by the NHS. All the other villas in the earlier view are still in place, although most are in a very run-down condition, being either in multiple occupancy or split as offices. Almost all those prominent chimney pots have gone, thanks to central heating.

NORMANTON ROAD

GIs OF THE US 82nd Airborne Division walk down Normanton Road towards Mill Hill Lane, 1944.
Normanton Road developed from a country lane in the 1860s and was widened in 1938–39
when Herbert Aslin built this extension to Derby Technical College (founded in Green Lane in
1878) on an awkward site, already in college occupation but home to a works that had been

redundant since 1924. As with the Council House, the outbreak of war prevented its completion. A four-storey L-shaped block, its height artfully broken by an attic cornice, was built almost next to Christ Church. A potentially handsome southward curving extension of twenty-five bays never got beyond the ground floor, and when money did become available a new start was made on Kedleston Road, now the university. (*Reproduced courtesy of* Derby Evening Telegraph)

THE UNIVERSITY (FOUNDED from disparate elements, including the technical college in 1992) declared Aslin's building redundant in 1996, and it was sold to developers Wheatcroft, who planned to create a retail park there. However, Mr Clinton Bourke, representing the developer, soon fell out with the council after his scheme was twice rejected on planning grounds. Unfortunately, by this time the college had been peremptorily demolished. The surviving building is the Ministry of Pensions' offices. Christ Church, sadly shorn of its pinnacles, is now Serbian Orthodox.

ST CHAD'S CHURCH

ST CHAD'S CHURCH, photographed by Richard Keene Ltd, 1899 (left). As this part of New Normanton expanded, churches were built. St Chad's named the road it stood upon, seen here at the junction of Mount Carmel Street with Gordon Road, where the Catholic Church of St Joseph, built by James Hart in 1897, also stood. St Chad's was built in 1882, the competition to design it being won by H.C. Turner. Behind the church are the schools. The interior of the church was very polychromatic with much carved alabaster by R.G. Lomas & Co. of Derby and wrought iron by Edwin Haslam, whose works adjoined those of Lomas.

THE CHURCH WAS demolished in 1990, its incumbent believing that the upkeep was too demanding and that with money raised by selling the site to a developer, a new, more manageable church could be built. Needless to say, it never happened; the site is still empty (but lent to the adjoining school) and the congregation seems to have melted away. Apart from a superfluity of motor cars, the scene is otherwise little changed.

RICHMOND LAUNDRY

RICHMOND LAUNDRY, CLARENCE Road, Normanton, 1909
(above and right). In 1908 Charles Frederick Pritchard, scion
of a family long involved in the manufacture of both brushes
and soft drinks, chose a location in Clarence Road to move
his Richmond Gold Medal Laundry to. He had Alexander

MacPherson of Derby (1847–1935) design this handsome brick building, which remained in dedicated use until the 1990s. The interior of the rear top-lit workshop at the Richmond Laundry 1908 can be seen on the top left. Laundering was a very labour-intensive industry, a fact borne out strikingly here. The mangles were driven by a steam engine.

WHEN THE RICHMOND Laundry works finally closed in 1999 they were bought by a local man who allowed the building to fall into some disrepair. However, the councillor for the area was positively ecstatic at having persuaded him to demolish the complex to build houses on the site (on the grounds that the building had become a danger to children playing (i.e. trespassing!)) despite the fact that it could so easily and attractively have been adapted into flats, or even 'prestige apartments'. The building was demolished in 2004 and replaced by these banal apartments (left) – what a waste of a good building.

EDWARDIAN SEMIS: BELVOIR STREET

BELVOIR STREET, NEW Normanton, *c.*1907. Originally intended by the developer, Joseph Porter of Spondon, to be called Lumley Street (after the castle and surname of the Earls of Scarbrough – hardly redolent with local associations), it and several neighbouring streets were eventually named after local hunts. Just out of view on the right is the Mafeking & Bowling Green inn, with a date

stone of 1900, thus dating the street, which runs from Porter Road (which the developer named after himself) to Clarence Road. (*Reproduced courtesy of Michael Allseybrook Esq.*)

BELVOIR STREET, 2011 (above). The houses are identical in plan, layout and detail to those in Porter Road, except that those in the latter are all terraced, whereas here all but four are in semi-detached pairs. They have sprouted satellite television aerials, UPVC windows, 'Kentucky' doors (also in UPVC) and motor cars. The iron railings on their dwarf brick walls were ripped out for the war effort in 1942, and now are mainly replaced by reconstituted stone. The vacant ground in the foreground of the older picture was dedicated in 1908 to the Clarence Road Schools (now Dale Primary), designed by the Belper firm of Hunter & Woodhouse. A remarkably handsome design, it has been ruined in the last twenty years by poorly designed and unsightly extensions.
(*Reproduced courtesy of Carole Craven*)

BURTON ROAD:
MOUNT CARMEL

BURTON ROAD, NOT long after
the tram route was electrified,
8 September 1904 (right).
From Littleover one returned to
Derby via Burton Road which,
on its final descent, passes
Mount Carmel, an elevated
residential enclave built on the
grounds of a long-vanished
house. The villas lining Burton
Road here date from the late
1880s and many are by Arthur
Eaton, including the one
with the turret (on the right).

Beyond it is the Moorish Mount Carmel Tower of 1869, actually the chimney of Mason's paint works. It was designed by Edwin Thompson (1801–83).
(*Reproduced courtesy of Michael Allseybrook Esq.*)

THE SCENE IS not much changed, for once, except that not long after the older photograph was taken the paint works closed and Mount Carmel Tower came down, to be replaced after the First World War by a motor garage. On the left, three villas have been connected together (to no good aesthetic effect) to create the International Hotel, which has been growing since its foundation in the 1950s. The turning (centre) is Breedon Hill Road, pitched in 1894.

BURTON ROAD AND GREEN LANE

BURTON ROAD, LITTLE City, *c*.1909. Little City was a very small enclave of some of the worst houses in Derby, situated at the top of Green Lane and built in about 1815. That part of it facing Burton Road, however, was more respectable, including part of the Tailors' Arms which, like the area itself, survived until 1960. Here the Normanton Road joins (left of the photograph)

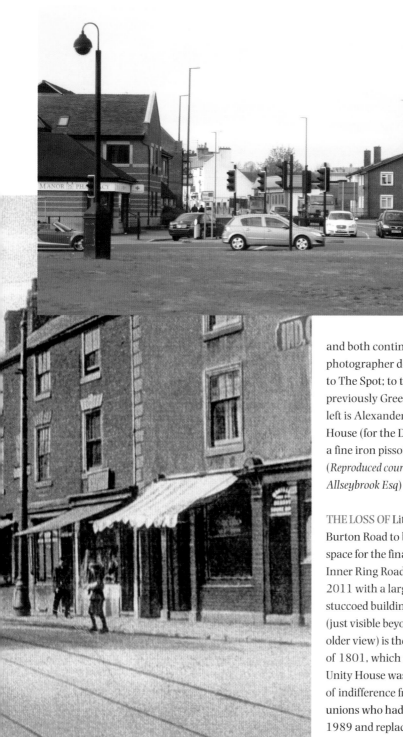

and both continue behind the photographer down Babington Lane to The Spot; to the right is Green Lane, previously Green Hill. Also on the left is Alexander MacPherson's Unity House (for the Derby TUC, 1908) and a fine iron pissoir. (*Reproduced courtesy of Michael Allseybrook Esq*)

THE LOSS OF Little City enabled Burton Road to be widened and gave space for the final section of the Derby Inner Ring Road to be completed in 2011 with a large roundabout. The stuccoed building in the distance (just visible beyond the tram in the older view) is the Bell & Castle Inn of 1801, which is still going strong. Unity House was demolished (to a tide of indifference from the local trades unions who had sold it long before) in 1989 and replaced by a combined GP surgery and retail pharmacy.

GRAND HOUSES IN GREEN LANE

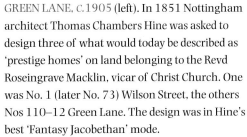

GREEN LANE, C.1905 (left). In 1851 Nottingham architect Thomas Chambers Hine was asked to design three of what would today be described as 'prestige homes' on land belonging to the Revd Roseingrave Macklin, vicar of Christ Church. One was No. 1 (later No. 73) Wilson Street, the others Nos 110–12 Green Lane. The design was in Hine's best 'Fantasy Jacobethan' mode.

AFTER THE FIRST World War this area ceased to be fashionable, and these houses were divided up, first as flats and then, after the Second World War, as office space. The two houses that comprised 110–12 Green Lane were sold in 2002 as office premises. Externally, though, little has changed in eighty years, whereas the interiors have been badly mauled, with the loss of cornicing, fireplaces and other details. The whole of the Green Lane area has been suggested as a conservation area, although so far it has taken the city council five years to deliberate upon the suggestion.

A CONVERTED CHAPEL

THE PRIMITIVE METHODIST chapel, photographed by Richard Keene Ltd in 1896: from this point upwards to Babington Lane, what today is Green Lane was, until a century ago, called Green Hill. This Italianate chapel was built in 1878 for the 'Prims' by Giles & Brookhouse of Derby. The strange thing is that it is an exact copy of the same partnership's long demolished Bourne chapel

in Kedleston Street, in Derby's old West End, built eight years before, presumably at the insistence of the Green Hill congregation.

IN THE TWENTIETH century the 'Prims' were re-absorbed by the Methodist movement, and by 1967 a dwindling and ageing congregation meant that the premises had to be sold. The purchaser was the proprietor of JB Furnishers, purveyors of 'G-plan' furniture. In adapting the building, wholesale slaughter of the interior, the removal of the pinnacles and the mauling of the lower part of the exterior were apparently necessary. The original 'Prims' would no doubt be turning in their graves if they knew that the building was currently an amusement arcade.

VICTORIA STREET

VICTORIA STREET, DECORATED
for a state visit by Queen Victoria,
21 May 1891 (right). The street
was created by the culverting of the
Markeaton Brook in 1837–39. On
the right is Robert Wallace's 1839
Athenaeum; ahead is the bulk of T.C.
Hine's Brookside (Congregational)
chapel of 1860. The lavish street
adornments were funded by the
mayor, maritime refrigeration
pioneer Sir Alfred Seale Haslam,
knighted that morning on platform
one of Derby station.
(*Reproduced courtesy of Derby
Museum*)

VICTORIA STREET, APRIL 2011 (left). The Athanaeum is still there, despite conversion in the 1950s into social security offices and re-conversion into a catering facility in 1987. The whole south side in the older view was replaced in 1962 by Ranby's department store, which became Debenhams but moved to Westfield in 2008, leaving the building half empty and half devoted to Silly Sid's furniture shop. Hine's chapel was also replaced in 1962, by an 'expresso machine'-faced brick box (centre), but the entire range is earmarked for redevelopment.

ST JAMES'S BRIDGE

THE ST JAMES'S AREA, 1907. The street to the right is The Strand, created in 1878 by Sir Abraham Woodiwiss by culverting the Markeaton Brook which once snaked through the town centre. The intersection was until then the site of St James's Bridge, built by the monks of the cell of St James, adjacent (part of Bermondsey Abbey), who charged a toll to cross it. The Derby architect William Giles designed the serpentine façade of the shops on The Strand (listed Grade II) as well as the 'flatiron' corner building two years later. The Wardwick is the street to the left.

THERE HAS BEEN remarkably little change since, except for the replacement of the two eighteenth-century buildings on the left. The three-bay one of 1932 is the former Saracen's Head, which later became an Irish-themed pub and is currently a bar called DGio's. Miraculously, the flatiron building has managed to retain all its exuberant iron brattishing on the roof and on its turrets. The streets hereabouts are now restricted to buses and taxis only.

ST JAMES'S STREET

ST JAMES'S STREET, Sunday 22 May 1932 (right). This was the worst flood since that of 1841 and, although there was no loss of life, millions of pounds of damage was caused as most businesses then stored their stock in cellars. The flood was caused – as Herbert Spencer had realised at the tender age of twenty in 1841 – by water backing up the swollen Derwent from the Trent and into the Markeaton Brook, itself in torrent. His solution – a movable barrier at Alvaston – was not accepted by the council until 1933, a wait of ninety-two years!

THE THREE-STOREY building in the centre of the image above is the former St James's Hotel of 1867, also by William Giles and opened in 1871. It closed in 1925–26, leaving merely a bar and restaurant on the ground floor. The ballroom became Richardson & Linnell's auction rooms for many decades. The remainder is now split into offices. The stone-clad building (right) is part of the general post office of 1869–71 designed by J. Williams (listed Grade II), which closed and moved in 2000, after which the building was converted into a bar.

VICTORIAN REDEVELOPMENT

NO. 21 THE WARDWICK, a previously unknown print by Keene. This building has now been replaced by the Susumi sushi bar. On the right is the former Allsopp town house of 1708, now the Wardwick Tavern. Although it has been difficult to determine much of its history, its elegant proportions and lack of detailing strongly suggest Joseph Pickford in his later years, c.1778–82. Originally it was intended as a town house. From 1852 to 1878 it was home to solicitor Henry H. Hutchinson.

THE SAME VIEW today, with No. 21 replaced by a much taller commercial building in the style of Giles & Brookhouse and erected in about 1879 for Linnells, drapers. The still lofty first-floor room was the County Club (see photograph on p. 90) for a long time, but after a long tenure by Golden Gains it became Susumi. No. 19–20 (Wardwick Tavern) has clearly had its shop fronting of the 1860s replaced by sash windows.

WARDWICK

THE WARDWICK TAKES its name from a lost medieval village, subsumed into the town in the eleventh century. The most prominent building shown is the so-called Jacobean House, built for

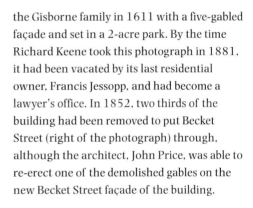

the Gisborne family in 1611 with a five-gabled façade and set in a 2-acre park. By the time Richard Keene took this photograph in 1881, it had been vacated by its last residential owner, Francis Jessopp, and had become a lawyer's office. In 1852, two thirds of the building had been removed to put Becket Street (right of the photograph) through, although the architect, John Price, was able to re-erect one of the demolished gables on the new Becket Street façade of the building.

THE SCENE HAS changed remarkably little 130 years on, apart from scaffolding temporarily enveloping the later seventeenth-century houses on either side of the Jacobean House. For most of the early twentieth century, the latter was a restaurant, but after the Second World War it became an estate agent's, which it remained until 2002, when it became a café bar which closed in 2010. Behind the Jacobean House, barely visible, is now an enormous office block in dark brick, built over what remained of its garden in the 1970s.

81

ST WERBURGH'S CHURCH

ST WERBURGH'S CHURCH, platinotype by Richard Keene, 1880s (right). This Saxon foundation, originally set within a small settlement called Wardwick but part of Derby by 1086, has had a chequered history. The medieval tower collapsed on 2 January 1601 and was replaced by 1608, as here, in an unaffectedly vernacular Gothic way. In 1698 most of the medieval nave collapsed and was replaced by the elegant baroque church also seen here. The nave was top-lit by a dome, but the architect is not known for sure. Note the cabbies' rest (right) in Cheapside.

ST WERBURGH'S, 2011 (above). In 1894 the church was again declared unsafe, and the nave was replaced by a new Gothic one on a non-liturgical alignment (to help obviate undermining by flooding), designed by Sir Arthur Blomfield (1829–99) and finished in 1898. The elegant

Regency Neo-Greek cast-iron railings visible here survived the rebuilding, but all bar a couple of panels were removed to build 'iron Spitfires' in 1942. The chancel was also left intact, with its Sir Francis Chantry monument, which is now in the care of the Churches Conservation Trust. The remainder, secularised in 1982 and briefly a shopping mall, has been derelict for thirteen years.

KING'S ARMS
COUNTY HOTEL

KING'S ARMS COUNTY Hotel, seen in a newly discovered Keene photograph, probably of 1877 (right). This hotel was added to the Shire Hall complex for the convenience of attorneys, plaintiffs and others attending the assizes. It was probably designed by the Improvement Commission's architect, Charles Finney (1773–1828), and was finished in 1798, with the sheriff's officer, John Webster, as the proprietor. On his death it was extended in a matching style. In this picture its 'Derby' windows (sashes paired under a single stone lintel) have already been reglazed in plate glass and the parapet has been rebuilt. The mystery is what it was like originally – the work was advertised as 'recent' in December 1876.
(*Reproduced courtesy of Michael J. Willis Esq.*)

THE BUILDING WAS turned into a library by the county council (which removed both original staircases and blocked the street entrance) in 1934 and in 1968 became a police station, which closed in 1988. It, the Shire Hall and the Judges' Lodgings – all part of a superbly elegant single complex – were then allowed to become derelict from 1994. Plans to convert the lot into thirteen magistrates' courts (far too many for such a complex) included the complete demolition of this building, but a vigorous campaign by Derby Civic Society against such destructive plans resulted in a reprieve, and it was adapted as part of the new courts (with a huge and ugly extension behind) in 2002–3.

THE THEATRE ROYAL

THEATRE ROYAL, BOLD Lane, sepia print by Samuel Hereford Parkins, after 1884. Very few satisfactory views of this interesting building survive before its façade of 1773 (attributed to Joseph Pickford for James Whiteley) was terribly mauled by that bastion of art and culture, Derbyshire County Council. After 1864 it was turned into a gospel hall by George Wilkins (a Dissenting printer). Compared with a very eccentric engraving of 1791, it stands up well. The building was, in fact, a converted maltings.
(*Reproduced courtesy of Derby Museum, Goodey Collection No. 157*)

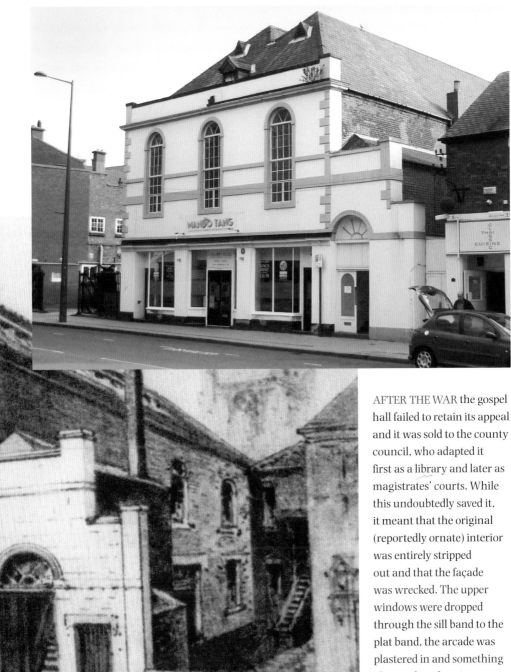

AFTER THE WAR the gospel hall failed to retain its appeal and it was sold to the county council, who adapted it first as a library and later as magistrates' courts. While this undoubtedly saved it, it meant that the original (reportedly ornate) interior was entirely stripped out and that the façade was wrecked. The upper windows were dropped through the sill band to the plat band, the arcade was plastered in and something akin to shop-fronting installed. In 2003 it became redundant and was put up for sale. It is now a Caribbean restaurant.

MRS PARKER'S HOUSE, FRIAR GATE

A 1712 DRAWING of Lower Friar Gate. This house was inhabited in her widowhood by Mrs Thomas Parker, mother of Lord Chancellor Thomas Parker, 1st Earl of Macclesfield (1666–1732), who was both Recorder of Derby from 1703 to 1710 and the borough's MP. The house was clearly timber-framed and jettied, and by 1712 it had been divided into four

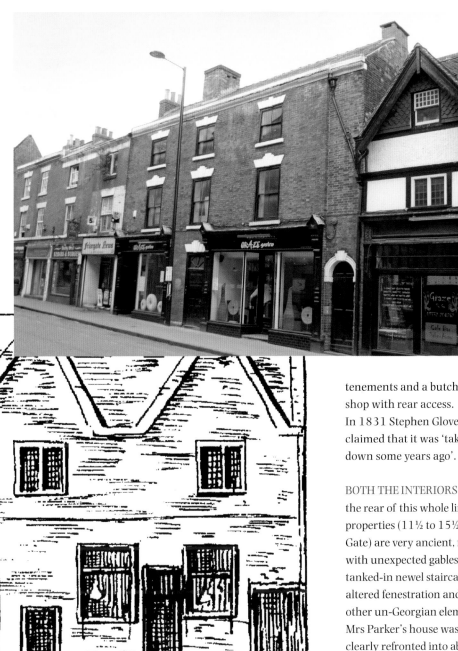

tenements and a butcher's shop with rear access. In 1831 Stephen Glover claimed that it was 'taken down some years ago'.

BOTH THE INTERIORS and the rear of this whole line of properties (11½ to 15½ Friar Gate) are very ancient, replete with unexpected gables, tanked-in newel staircases, altered fenestration and other un-Georgian elements. Mrs Parker's house was clearly refronted into about three separate buildings; the rainwater hopper nearest the camera carries the date 1806, which about fits the period. These properties badly need listing.

THE FORMER
COUNTY CLUB

NO. 103 FRIAR Gate, 1963 (right). The Portland Temperance Club was in residence here until 1922, when, as a result of the loss of financial support from the widowed Mrs Boden of The Friary, who moved to Chard, the club was forced to move out. The County Club, which had been housed at No. 21 The Wardwick, bought it after this. Before the 1890s it had been a private house, a very severe Regency building with a façade full of Derby windows, much like the King's Arms County Hotel (see pictures on p.84–85), and it may thus be tentatively attributed to Charles Finney and dated to about 1795–1800. (*Reproduced courtesy of Don Farnsworth*)

IN 1971–72 THE club and the 1694 Presbyterian chapel next door were demolished in order to clear space for a vast and inappropriate office development by T.H. Thorpe & Partners sponsored by Viking Properties and mockingly called Heritage Gate, most of which remained untenanted for well over a decade. The promoters were rather bailed out when the city council acquired Roman House – the part on the site of the County Club – in 1988. The four-storey street front here is in a banal sub-Georgian pastiche with an ersatz Doric portico representing what can politely be called a playful use of the orders.

A HOUSE IN FRIAR GATE

BRIDGE STREET, 1887 (right). This building was built as a result of the First Derby Improvement Act of 1768, and is attributable to the architect Joseph Pickford. It is two houses, a two-bay one facing Friar Gate (left of the photograph) and a three-bay south-facing one – seen here decorated for Queen Victoria's Golden Jubilee in 1887 – its offset entrance is reached through a garden to the side facing the camera. The Third Improvement Act, however, which allowed the sale of Nuns' Green, resulted in the pitching of Bridge Street through it in 1793, putting the entrance virtually on the pavement.

THE SAME SCENE in April 2011 (above). Little has changed, except that the house was altered for two surgeons in 1900 to designs by Percy Currey. The rear extension, probably erected in 1793, has had a modest ground-floor part added to a canted stair tower placed where the extension joins the house, and the entrance has been rebuilt with an Ionic portico, one side of which is supported by a rusticated pillar. Modern plumbing has marred the well-proportioned façade and the elegant plain railings of 1793 were ripped up in 1942. The road outside, now part of a one-way system, is like a race track – surely no way to treat one's premier conservation area.

THE ASHBOURNE ROAD

ASHBOURNE ROAD, *c.*1909. This is looking west from the corner of Fowler Street; note the impressive row of middling quality Regency villas that line the north side, No. 28 is nearest

the camera. Almost behind the tramway catenary support (centre of the photograph) is the oddly designed No. 39, with No. 40, home of that indefatigable patron of Derby topographical art, Alfred E. Goodey (1869–1945), beyond.

A VIEW JUST slightly further along in April 2011 (above). The house, far right, has been recently converted into luxury apartments, and a vast modern complex is attached behind it. The house just visible beyond it, now a nursery, was the long-term home of Alfred E. Goodey who commissioned many local artists to paint parts of Derby, especially where older buildings were falling to the developer's ball and chain. He gave over 500 of these to Derby Museum in 1936.

Other titles published by The History Press

Haunted Derbyshire

JILL ARMITAGE

Haunted Derbyshire contains many creepy accounts of spirits, spectres and poltergeists - including the Mad Monk of North Wingfield, the crying angel of Etwell and the headless ghost of Wenley Hill. If you have ever wondered why the Chesterfield Canal veered from its straight course, why horses shy at crossroads, empty theatre seats move or miners leave shoes in mines, *Haunted Derbyshire* will give you the chilling answers.

978 0 7524 4886 2

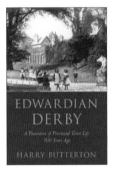

Edwardian Derby

HARRY BUTTERTON

Situated in the industrial heartland of Britain, Derby had played an important role in the Industrial Revolution of the Victorian era, but how would it fare in the new century? All aspects of daily life in Derby are covered; providing a fascinating glimpse into a lost world. Copiously illustrated with more than 100 images and full of intriguing insights, *Edwardian Derby* has something for everyone – young, old, visitor and resident alike – who has an interest in the City of Derby and would like to know more about its complex past.

978 0 7524 4702 5

Romantic Haunts of Derbyshire

JILL ARMITAGE

Since the days of Jane Austen, Derbyshire has been considered one of England's most romantic destinations but unfortunately not everyone is as lucky in love as Elizabeth Bennet. From creepy sightings of mysterious shadowy figures and spirits, such as the kissing ghost at Renishaw Hall, to moving objects, unexplained sounds and bloodstains that cannot be removed, this selection covers various aspects of paranormal – and romantic – activity in the county.

978 0 7524 4651 6

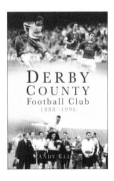

Derby County FC

ANDY ELLIS

Derby County, one of the Football League's founding clubs in 1888, has a rich and colourful existence that reflects the fortunes of an archetypal English football club. Andy Ellis has collated all of this drama into one book containing over 200 photographs –many of them unseen for several decades and some previously unpublished – that reveal the character of one of Britain's most iconic clubs.

978 0 7524 4792 6

Visit our website and discover thousands of other History Press books.

www.thehistorypress.co.uk

The History Press